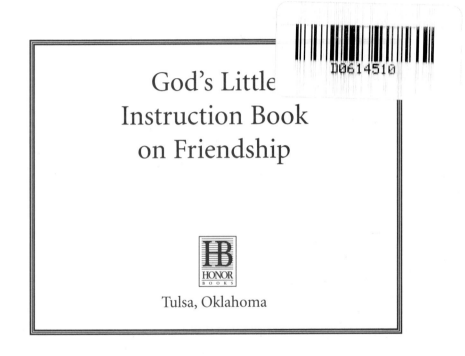

God's Little Instruction Book on Friendship

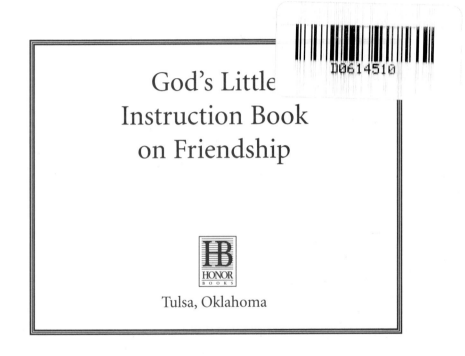

HB
HONOR
BOOKS

Tulsa, Oklahoma

God's Little Instruction Book on Friendship
ISBN 1-56292-078-2
Copyright © 1996 by Honor Books, Inc.
P. O. Box 55388
Tulsa, Oklahoma 74155

9th Printing

Manuscript prepared by W. B. Freeman Concepts, Inc., Tulsa, Oklahoma

INTRODUCTION

A genuine friend is one who is there for you at all times — someone who believes in you even if they do not understand or approve of what you do. That is the type of Friend Jesus is to those who follow Him.

This book speaks of the blessing of friendship, but also of how to choose a friend and be a friend. When Jesus is at the center of a friendship, that relationship will last and become stronger and more precious through the years.

As you make Jesus your number-one Friend and pursue friendships with others, you will soon discover that you not only have a wonderful support group in time of need, but a great deal more fun along life's way.

Today a man discovered gold
and fame,
Another flew the stormy seas;
Another set an unarmed world
aflame,
One found the germ of a disease.
But what high fates my path
attend:
For I — today I found a friend.

*Make to
yourselves friends.
Luke 16:9*

*You prepare
a table before
me....You anoint
my head with oil;
my
cup runs over.
Psalm 23:5 NKJV*

We cannot tell the precise moment when friendship is formed. As in filling a vessel drop by drop, there is at last a drop which makes it run over; so in a series of kindnesses there is at last one which makes the heart run over.

How rare and wonderful is that flash of a moment when we realize we have discovered a friend.

O Lord, Thou hast searched me and known me ...such knowledge is too wonderful for me.
Psalm 139:1, 6
NASB

7

A good name is better than precious ointment, And the day of death than the day of one's birth.
Ecclesiastes 7:1
NKJV

And I can live my life on earth
Contented to the end,
If but a few shall know my worth
And proudly call me friend.

A true friend unbosoms freely, advises justly, assists readily, adventures boldly, takes all patiently, defends courageously, and continues a friend unchangeably.

If you love someone you will be loyal to him no matter what the cost. You will always believe in him, always expect the best of him, and always stand your ground in defending him.
1 Corinthians 13:7 TLB

Let not mercy and truth forsake you; bind them around your neck, write them on the tablet of your heart, and so find favor and high esteem in the sight of God and man.

Proverbs 3:3-4

NKJV

To have a good friend is one of the highest delights of life; to be a good friend is one of the noblest and most difficult undertakings.

Do not keep the alabaster boxes of your love and tenderness sealed up until your friends are dead. Fill their lives with sweetness. Speak approvingly cheering words while their ears can hear them and while their hearts can be thrilled by them.

How sweet are thy words unto my taste! yea, sweeter than honey to my mouth!
Psalm 119:103

My friends have made the story of my life. In a thousand ways they have turned my limitations into beautiful privileges, and enabled me to walk serene and happy in the shadow cast by my deprivation.

Each one helps the other, saying to one another, "Take courage!"
Isaiah 41:6 NRSV

And I will gladly share with you your pain,
If it turns out I can no comfort bring;
For 'tis a friend's right, please let me explain,
To share in woful as in joyful things.

They laid hold upon one Simon, a Cyrenian... and on him they laid the cross, that he might bear it after Jesus.
Luke 23:26

A mirror reflects a man's face, but what he is really like is shown by the kind of friends he chooses.
Proverbs 27:19
TLB

The best mirror is an old friend.

14

A faithful friend is an image of God.

But we all, as with unveiled face we see as in a mirror the Lord's glory reflected, are changed into the same likeness from one degree of glory to another.
2 Corinthians 3:18 MLB

...and that not of yourselves; it is the gift of God.
Ephesians 2:8
NKJV

I no doubt deserved my enemies, but I don't believe I deserved my friends.

Friendship improves happiness, and abates misery, by doubling our joy, and dividing our grief.

You are a garden fountain, a well of living water, refreshing as the streams from the Lebanon mountains.
Song of Solomon 4:15 TLB

God has placed the members, each one of them, in the body, just as He desired. And if they were all one member, where would the body be?
1 Corinthians 12:18-19 NASB

Brotherhood is the very price and condition of man's survival.

Every man should have a fair sized cemetery in which to bury the faults of his friends.

Who can discern his errors? Forgive my hidden faults.
Psalm 19:12 NIV

Love your enemies, do good to those who hate you, bless those who curse you, pray for those who abuse you.
Luke 6:27-28
NRSV

Am I not destroying my enemies when I make friends of them?

20

Anyone with a heart full of friendship has a hard time finding enemies.

You must love your neighbor just as much as you love yourself.
Luke 10:27 TLB

H e who gets and never gives
Will lose the truest friend
    that lives;
He who gives and never gets
Will sour his friendships
    with regrets;
Giving and getting, thus alone
A friendship lives — or dies
    a-moan!

But do not forget to do good and to share, for with such sacrifices God is well pleased.
Hebrews 13:16
NKJV

Friendship hath the skill and observation of the best physician, the diligence and vigilance of the best nurse, and the tenderness and patience of the best mother.

I have become all things to all men, that I might by all means save some.
1 Corinthians 9:22 NKJV

How can one be warm alone?
Ecclesiastes 4:11
NASB

A true friend is the gift of God, and he only who made hearts can unite them.

The impulse of love that leads us to the doorway of a friend is the voice of God within.

Whether you turn to the right or to the left, your ears will hear a voice behind you, saying, "This is the way; walk in it." Isaiah 30:21 NIV

*Rejoice with those
who rejoice.
Romans 12:15
NKJV*

Anybody can sympathize with the sufferings of a friend, but it requires a very fine nature to sympathize with a friend's success.

It is one of the severest tests of friendship to tell your friend his faults. So to love a man that you cannot bear to see a stain upon him, and to speak painful truth through loving words, that is friendship.

Faithful are the wounds of a friend; but the kisses of an enemy are deceitful.
Proverbs 27:6

He who covers and forgives an offense seeks love, but he who repeats or harps on a matter separates even close friends.
Proverbs 17:9
AMP

Far better 'twere for either to be mute, Than for to murder friendship by dispute.

Since there is nothing so well worth having as friends, never lose a chance to make them.

As occasion and opportunity open up to us, let us do good [morally] to all people [not only being useful or profitable to them, but also doing what is for their spiritual good and advantage].
Galatians 6:10
AMP

29

Julius was very good to Paul and gave him freedom to go visit his friends, who took care of his needs.
Acts 27:3 NCV

Instead of herds of oxen, endeavor to assemble flocks of friends about your house.

True friendship is a plant of slow growth, and must undergo and withstand the shocks of adversity before it is entitled to the appelation.

And let us not be weary in well doing: for in due season we shall reap, if we faint not.
Galatians 6:9

31

Do not forsake me when my strength fails. For my enemies speak against me.
Psalm 71:9-10
NKJV

Strength wains when your enemies speak against you, but weakness is strong when your friends stand by you.

Happy is the house that shelters a friend.

And when she was baptized, and her household, she besought us, saying, If ye have judged me to be faithful to the Lord, come into my house, and abide there.
Acts 16:15

A rope that is woven of three strings is hard to break.
Ecclesiastes 4:12
NCV

Christian friendship is a triple-braided cord.

I s any pleasure on earth as great as a circle of Christian friends by a fire?

How very good and pleasant it is when kindred live together in unity! Psalm 133:1 NRSV

So in Christ we who are many form one body, and each member belongs to all the others.
Romans 12:5 NIV

The bird, a nest; the spider, a web; man, friendship.

Who seeks a faultless friend remains friendless.

He who covers a transgression seeks love.
Proverbs 17:9
NKJV

Brother, if someone is caught in a sin, you who are spiritual should restore him gently.
Galatians 6:1 NIV

It is prudent to pour the oil of delicate politeness on the machinery of friendship.

Silences make the real conversations between friends. Not the saying but the never needing to say is what counts.

Deep calls to deep.
Psalm 42:7 NASB

If your enemy is hungry, feed him; if he is thirsty, give him something to drink... overcome evil with good.
Romans 12:20-21

Love is the only force capable of transforming an enemy into a friend.

40

Promises may get friends, but it is performance that must nurse and keep them.

But do you want to know, O foolish man, that faith without works is dead?
James 2:20 NKJV

Therefore, if anyone is in Christ, he is a new creation; old things have passed away; behold, all things have become new.
2 Corinthians 5:17 NKJV

Each friend represents a world in us, a world possibly not born until they arrive, and it is only by this meeting that a new world is born.

The meeting of two personalities is like the contact of two chemical substances...if there are any reactions, both are transformed.

Let us pursue the things which make for peace and the things by which one may edify another.
Romans 14:19
NKJV

There should be no division in the body, but that the members should have the same care for one another.
1 Corinthians 12:25 NASB

Friendship is more delicate than love.

When my friends are one-eyed, I look at their profile.

Think about things that are pure and lovely, and dwell on the fine, good things in others.
Philippians 4:8
TLB

*A friend loves
at all times.
Proverbs 17:17
NKJV*

Friendships are fragile things, and require as much care in handling as any other fragile and precious thing.

T he best way to keep your friends is not to give them away.

May the Lord make us keep our promises to each other, for he has witnessed them.
1 Samuel 20:23
TLB

*There is a friend
who sticks closer
than a brother.
Proverbs 18:24
NIV*

Old friends are best. King James used to call for his old shoes; they were the easiest for his feet.

A h, how good it feels!
The hand of
an old friend.

You open Your hand and satisfy the desire of every living thing.
Psalm 145:16
NKJV

*A friend nearby
is better than
relatives far away.
Proverbs 27:10
CEV*

Something like home that is not home is to be desired; it is found in the house of a friend.

"Stay" is a charming word in a friend's vocabulary.

Be content, I pray thee, and tarry all night, and let thine heart be merry.
Judges 19:6

There was once a pretty chicken, but his friends were pretty few,
For he thought that there was nothing in the world but what he knew.

I want not a friend servilely to comply with all my humors and fancies, and ever be obedient to my nod, for my shadow does as much as this, but I want one who will follow me only in obedience to truth, and assist me impartially with his judgment.

The sweetness of a man's friend gives delight by hearty counsel.
Proverbs 27:9
NKJV

Whosoever therefore will be a friend of the world is the enemy of God.
James 4:4

A friend to all is a friend to none.

Who ceases to be
a friend,
never was one.

*This people
honors Me with
their lips, but
their heart is far
away from Me.*
Mark 7:6-7 NASB

Whatever you did for one of the least of these brothers of mine, you did for me.
Matthew 25:40
NIV

He does good to himself who does good to his friend.

A friend in need is a friend indeed.

I will exult and rejoice in your steadfast love, because you have seen my affliction; you have taken heed of my adversities.
Psalm 31:7 NRSV

Can two walk together, unless they are agreed?
Amos 3:3 NKJV

Friendship is a union of spirits.

What is a friend? A single soul dwelling in two bodies.

The soul of Jonathan was knit to the soul of David, and Jonathan loved him as his own soul.
1 Samuel 18:1
NKJV

Esteem them very highly in love for their work's sake.
1 Thessalonians 5:13 NKJV

Convey thy love to thy friend, as an arrow to the mark, to stick there; not as a ball against the wall to rebound back to thee.

There was a definite process by which one made people into friends, and it involved talking to them and listening to them for hours at a time.

My dear brothers and sisters, always be willing to listen and slow to speak.
James 1:19 NCV

I rejoice that in everything I have confidence in you.
2 Corinthians 7:16 NASB

A friend is a person with whom I may be sincere. Before him, I may think aloud.

The essence of true friendship is to make allowance for another's little lapses.

Honor God by accepting each other, as Christ has accepted you.
Romans 15:7 CEV

Do not merely look out for your own personal interests, but also for the interests of others.
Philippians 2:4
NASB

Friendship is a strong and habitual inclination in two persons to promote the good and happiness of one another.

Treat your friends as you do your picture, and place them in their best light.

Love...is ever ready to believe the best of every person.
1 Corinthians 13:7 AMP

May the Lord cause you to increase and abound in love for one another.
1 Thessalonians 3:12 NASB

Friendship with the good is like the evening shadows, increasing till the sun of life sets.

The making of friends, who are real friends, is the best token we have of a man's success in life.

A righteous man will be remembered forever.
Psalm 112:6 NIV

I pray that the Lord will be kind to the family of Onesiphorus. He often cheered me up and wasn't ashamed of me when I was put in jail.
2 Timothy 1:16
CEV

A real friend is one who walks in when the rest of the world walks out.

The friends thou hast and their adoption tried, grapple them to thy soul with hooks of steel.

Hold fast to that which is good.
1 Thessalonians
5:21 NASB

*We do all things,
dearly beloved, for
your edifying.
2 Corinthians
12:19*

No man is useless while he is a friend.

Long ago I made up my mind to let my friends have their peculiarities.

Keep fervent in your love for one another, because love covers a multitude of sins.
1 Peter 4:8 NASB

Finally, let all of you be harmonious, sympathetic, loving as brothers, compassionate, humbleminded.
1 Peter 3:8 MLB

People are lonely because they build walls instead of bridges.

Imitating Christ is opening the door to friendship.

Be therefore imitators of God as His beloved children, and live in love, as Christ also loved us and gave Himself for us.
Ephesians 5:1-2
MLB

Honor one another above yourselves.
Romans 12:10
NIV

Y ou can make more friends in two months by becoming more interested in other people than you can in two years by trying to get people interested in you.

L ead the life that will make you kindly and friendly to every one about you, and you will be surprised what a happy life you will live.

He that hath a bountiful eye shall be blessed.
Proverbs 22:9

He who is faithful in what is least is faithful also in much; and he who is unjust in what is least is unjust also in much.
Luke 16:10 NKJV

He who is true to one friend thus proves himself worthy of many.

The man who treasures his friends is usually solid gold himself.

Now that you have purified yourselves by obeying the truth so that you have sincere love for your brothers, love one another deeply, from the heart.
1 Peter 1:22 NIV

The Lord your God has chosen you out of all the peoples on the face of the earth to be his people, his treasured possession... because the Lord loved you.
Deuteronomy 7:6,8 NIV

I keep my friends as misers do their treasure, because of all the things granted us by wisdom, none is greater or better than friendship.

Friendship renders prosperity more brilliant, while it lightens adversity by sharing it and making its burden common.

Rejoice with them that do rejoice, and weep with them that weep.
Romans 12:15

I thank my God upon every remembrance of you...I have you in my heart.
Philippians 1:3,7
NKJV

Think where man's glory most begins and ends
And say that my glory was I had such friends.

The supreme happiness of life is the conviction of being loved for yourself, or, more correctly, being loved in spite of yourself.

But God commendeth his love toward us, in that, while we were yet sinners, Christ died for us.
Romans 5:8

Do not correct a scoffer, lest he hate you; rebuke a wise man, and he will love you.
Proverbs 9:8 NKJV

Reprove a friend in secret, but praise him before others.

To speak painful truth through loving words is friendship.

You can trust a friend who corrects you.
Proverbs 27:6 CEV

But if we walk in the light, as he is in the light, we have fellowship with one another.
1 John 1:7 NIV

Having and being a friend means wanting only the best for each other.

My only sketch, profile, of Heaven is a large blue sky...larger than the biggest I have seen in June — and in it are my friends — every one of them.

But now that Timothy has come to us from you, and brought us good news of your faith and love, and that you always have good remembrance of us, greatly desiring to see us, as we also to see you.
1 Thessalonians 3:6 NKJV

Blessed is the man who does not walk in the counsel of the wicked or stand in the way of sinners or sit in the seat of mockers. But his delight is in the law of the Lord.
Psalm 1:1-2 NIV

No one should ever go on a journey with any other than him with whom one walks arm in arm, in the evening, the twilight, and agrees that if either should have a son he shall be named after the other.

No distance of place or lapse of time can lessen the friendship of those who are thoroughly persuaded of each other's worth.

For I am persuaded, that neither death, nor life, nor angels, nor principalities, nor powers, nor things present, nor things to come, nor height, nor depth, nor any other creature, shall be able to separate us from the love of God, which is in Christ Jesus our Lord.

Romans 8:38-39

Jonathan told David, saying, "Saul my father is seeking to put you to death. Now therefore, please be on guard in the morning, and stay in a secret place and hide yourself."
1 Samuel 19:2
NASB

True friends are a sure refuge.

It is in the shelter of each other that the people live.

I long to dwell in your tent forever and take refuge in the shelter of your wings.
Psalm 61:4 NIV

*A faithful
ambassador
brings health.
Proverbs 13:17
NKJV*

A faithful friend is the medicine of life.

Loyalty is what we seek in friendship.

If you love someone you will be loyal to him no matter what the cost. You will always believe in him, always expect the best of him, and always stand your ground in defending him.
1 Corinthians 13:7 TLB

Elisha said unto [Elijah], As the Lord liveth, and as thy soul liveth, I will not leave thee.
2 Kings 2:2

Be slow in choosing a friend, slower in changing.

He that lies down with dogs shall rise up with fleas.

The companion of fools will suffer harm.
Proverbs 13:20
NASB

A perverse man sows strife, and a whisperer separates the best of friends.
Proverbs 16:28
NKJV

Nothing is more dangerous than a friend without discretion; even a prudent enemy is preferable.

D̲o not remove a fly from your friend's forehead with a hatchet.

Convince, rebuke, and encourage, with the utmost patience in teaching.
2 Timothy 4:2
NRSV

Then some people came, bringing to him a paralyzed man, carried by four of them.
Mark 2:3 NRSV

When a friend is in trouble, don't annoy him by asking if there is anything you can do. Think up something appropriate and do it.

Actions, not words, are the true criterion of the attachment of friends.

Let us not love with words or tongue but with actions and in truth.
1 John 3:18 NIV

If they fall, the one will lift up his fellow.
Ecclesiastes 4:10

There is nothing so great that I fear to do it for my friend; nothing so small that I will disdain to do it for him.

He is our friend who loves more than admires us, and would aid us in our great work.

May the God of peace... equip you with everything good for doing his will...
Hebrews 13:20-21
NIV

The man of many friends...will prove himself a bad friend.
Proverbs 18:24
AMP

There is scarcity of friendship, but not of friends.

100

We inherit our relatives and our features and may not escape them; but we can select our clothing and our friends, and let us be careful that both fit us well.

Be ye not unequally yoked together with unbelievers: for what fellowship hath righteousness with unrighteousness? and what communion hath light with darkness? 2 Corinthians 6:14

Iron sharpeneth iron; so a man sharpeneth the countenance of his friend.
Proverbs 27:17

We are advertis'd by our loving friends.

102

Keep well thy tongue and keep thy friends.

Whoso keepeth his mouth and his tongue keepeth his soul from troubles.
Proverbs 21:23

Let each of you look not to your own interests, but to the interests of others.
Philippians 2:4
NRSV

Blessed are they who have the gift of making friends, for it is one of God's best gifts. It involves many things, but above all, the power of getting out of one's self, and appreciating whatever is noble and loving in another.

(Friendship is) the inexpressible comfort of feeling safe with a person, having neither to weigh thoughts nor measure words.

Guard and keep the harmony and oneness of (and produced by) the Spirit.
Ephesians 4:3
AMP

Do good, and lend, expecting nothing in return; and your reward will be great.
Luke 6:35 NASB

I do then with my friends as I do with my books. I would have them where I can find them, but I seldom use them.

A friend that you have to buy won't be worth what you pay for him, no matter what that may be.

He who is greedy for gain troubles his own house.
Proverbs 15:27
NKJV

There is no friend like a sister
In calm or stormy weather;
To cheer one on the tedious
    way,
To fetch one if one goes astray,
To lift one if one totters down,
To strengthen whilst one stands.

I behaved myself as though he had been my friend or brother.
Psalm 35:14

No medicine is more valuable, none more efficacious, none better suited to the cure of all our temporal ills than a friend to whom we may turn for consolation in time of trouble, and with whom we may share our happiness in time of joy.

Thy words were found and... became for me a joy and the delight of my heart.
Jeremiah 15:16
NASB

As the Lord lives, and as my lord the king lives, wherever my lord the king may be, whether for death or for life, there also your servant will be.
2 Samuel 15:21
NRSV

Trouble is a sieve through which we sift our acquaintances. Those too big to pass through are our friends.

110

Tell me whom you frequent, and I will tell you who you are.

He who walks with wise men will be wise.
Proverbs 13:20
NKJV

For the despairing man there should be kindness from his friend.
Job 6:14 NASB

There are deep sorrows and killing cares in life, but the encouragement and love of friends were given us to make all difficulties bearable.

It is not so much our friends' help that helps us, as the confidence of their help.

I am confident about you in the Lord.
Galatians 5:10
NRSV

I have come to have much joy and comfort in your love.
Philemon 1:7
NASB

Without friends no one would choose to live, though he had all other goods.

A real friend helps us think our best thoughts, do our noblest deeds, be our finest selves.

Friend, go up higher.
Luke 14:10

David met Jonathan, the king's son, and there was an immediate bond of love between them. Jonathan swore to be his blood brother.
1 Samuel 18:1-2
TLB

There is magic in the memory of schoolboy friendships; it softens the heart.

There can never be any solid friendship between individuals...unless the parties be persuaded of each other's honesty.

I have no greater joy than this, to hear of my children walking in the truth.
3 John 4 NASB

117

Greater love has no one than this, than to lay down one's life for his friends.
John 15:13 NKJV

If we would build on a sure foundation in friendship, we must love our friends for their sakes rather than for our own.

Keep the other person's well-being in mind when you feel an attack of soul-purging truth coming on.

Speaking the truth in love.
Ephesians 4:15
NASB

If one prevail against him, two shall withstand him.
Ecclesiastes 4:12

The most I can do for my friend is simply to be his friend.

A man, sir, should keep his friendship in constant repair.

If you bring your gift to the altar, and there remember that your brother has something against you, leave your gift there before the altar, and go your way. First be reconciled to your brother, and then come and offer your gift.
Matthew 5:23-24
NKJV

If a man falls when he is alone, he's in trouble.
Ecclesiastes 4:10
TLB

There is no wilderness like a life without friends.

122

Best friend, my well-spring in the wilderness!

The Lord will guide you always; he will satisfy your needs in a sun-scorched land ...You will be like a well-watered garden, like a spring whose waters never fail.
Isaiah 58:11 NIV

The years between
  Have taught me some
    sweet,
Some bitter lessons; none
Wiser than this — to
Spend in all things else,
But of old friends,
Be most miserly.

Let love be without hypocrisy. Abhor what is evil; cling to what is good.
Romans 12:9
NASB

124

Friends — the young they keep out of mischief; to the old they are a comfort and aid in their weakness, and those in the prime of life they incite to noble deeds.

We took sweet counsel together, and walked unto the house of God in company.
Psalm 55:14

You should take care of the needs of those who are troubled.... Then you will find joy in the Lord.
Isaiah 58:10,14
NCV

All who would win joy, must share it; happiness was born a twin.

But every road is rough to me that has no friend to cheer it.

You are better off to have a friend than to be all alone, because then you will get more enjoyment out of what you earn.
Ecclesiastes 4:9
CEV

And we urge you brothers... encourage the timid, help the weak, be patient with everyone.
1 Thessalonians 5:14 NIV

If the first law of friendship is that it has to be cultivated, the second law is to be indulgent when the first law has been neglected.

To preserve a friend three things are necessary; to honor him present, praise him absent, and assist him in his necessities.

Give you brothers and sisters more honor than you want for yourselves. Share with God's people who need help.
Romans 12:10,13
NCV

129

Then Jonathan said to David, "Go in peace, since we have both sworn in the name of the Lord, saying, 'May the Lord be between you and me, and between your descendants and my descendants, forever.'"
1 Samuel 20:42
NKJV

The truth is, friendship is to me every bit as sacred and eternal as marriage.

Friendship, of itself
a holy tie,
Is made more sacred
by adversity.

*A true friend
is always loyal,
and a brother is
born to help in
time of need.*
Proverbs 17:17
TLB

By the blessing of the upright a city is exalted.
Proverbs 11:11
NASB

Life has no blessing like a prudent friend.

The cunning seldom
gain their ends;
The wise are never
without friends.

And the Lord
spake unto Moses
face to face, as a
man speaketh
unto his friend.
Exodus 33:11

Many people claim to be loyal. But it is hard to find someone who really can be trusted.
Proverbs 20:6
NCV

One does not make friends; one recognizes them.

Friend is a word of Royal tone
Friend is a Poem all alone.

He who loves a pure heart and whose speech is gracious will have the king for his friend.
Proverbs 22:11
NIV

135

All who believed were together and had all things in common; they would sell their possessions and goods and distribute the proceeds to all, as any had need.
Acts 2:44-45
NRSV

Friendship is in loving rather than in being loved.

Friendship is the finest balm for the pangs of despised love.

As he sat at meat, there came a woman having an alabaster box of ointment of spikenard very precious; and she brake the box, and poured it on his head...and Jesus said, Let her alone...she hath wrought a good work on me.
Mark 14:3,6

I sought the Lord, and he heard me.
Psalm 34:4

The most called-upon prerequisite of a friend is an accessible ear.

Your wealth is where your friends are.

For where your treasure is, there your heart will be also.
Matthew 6:21
NRSV

Therefore comfort each other and edify one another, just as you also are doing.
1 Thessalonians 5:11 NKJV

Warm friendship like the setting sun shines kindly light on everyone.

140

I have three chairs in my house: one for solitude, two for friendship, three for company.

Where two or three gather together because they are mine, I will be right there among them.
Matthew 18:20
TLB

Every good thing bestowed and every perfect gift is from above, coming down from the Father.
James 1:17 NASB

Heaven gives us friends to bless the present scene.

142

True friendship...is infinite and immortal.

I have loved you with an everlasting love; therefore I have drawn you with lovingkindness.
Jeremiah 31:3
NASB

O Lord, you have searched me and you know me.... You are familiar with all my ways.
Psalm 139:1,3
NIV

A friend is someone with whom you can be one-hundred percent yourself.

Friendship is the only thing in the world concerning the usefulness of which all mankind are agreed.

The whole body, being fitted and held together by that which every joint supplies, according to the proper working of each individual part, causes the growth of the body for the building up of itself in love.
Ephesians 4:16
NASB

The righteous should choose his friends carefully, for the way of the wicked leads them astray.
Proverbs 12:26
NKJV

The true happiness consists not in the multitude of friends, but in their worth and choice.

You become who your friends are.

Those who believed were of one heart and one soul.
Acts 4:32 NKJV

*The Lord your
God is with you
...he will quiet
you with his love.
Zephaniah 3:17
NIV*

True friendship comes when silence between two people is comfortable.

148

A real friend is a person who, when you've made a fool of yourself, lets you forget it.

Love forgets mistakes; nagging about them parts the best of friends.
Proverbs 17:9 TLB

Do not save your loving speeches
For your friends till they are dead;
Do not write them on their tombstones,
Speak them rather now instead.

Be kind to this people, and please them, and speak good words to them.
2 Chronicles 10:7

By friendship you mean the greatest love, the greatest usefulness, the most open communication, the noblest sufferings, the severest truth, the heartiest counsel, and the greatest union of minds of which brave men and women are capable.

I have called you friends, for all things that I have heard from My Father I have made known to you.
John 15:15 NASB

The lintel low enough to keep out pomp and pride; the threshold high enough to turn deceit aside; the doorband strong enough from robbers to defend: this door will open at a touch to welcome every friend.

Love does no harm to a neighbor.
Romans 13:10
NKJV

Friendship is the source of the greatest pleasures, and without friends even the most agreeable pursuits become tedious.

These only are my fellowworkers unto the kingdom of God, which have been a comfort unto me.
Colossians 4:11

Do not urge me to leave you or turn back from following you; for where you go, I will go, and where you lodge, I will lodge. Your people shall be my people, and your God, my God.
Ruth 1:16 NASB

The reward of friendship is itself. The man who hopes for anything else does not understand what true friendship is.

References

Unless otherwise indicated, all Scripture quotations are taken from the *King James Version* of the Bible.

Scripture quotations marked NKJV are taken from *The New King James Version* of the Bible. Copyright © 1979, 1980, 1982, 1994 by Thomas Nelson, Inc., Publishers. Used by permission.

Scripture quotations marked NASB are taken from the *New American Standard Bible.* Copyright © The Lockman Foundation 1960, 1962, 1963, 1968, 1971, 1972, 1973, 1975, 1977. Used by permission.

Scripture quotations marked NIV are taken from the *Holy Bible, New International Version*® NIV®. Copyright © 1973, 1978, 1984 by International Bible Society. Used by permission of Zondervan Publishing House. All rights reserved.

Scripture quotations marked NRSV are taken from *The New Revised Standard Version Bible*, copyright © 1989 by the Division of Christian Education of the Churches of Christ in the United States of America and is used by permission.

Acknowledgements

We acknowledge and thank the following people for the quotes used in this book: Helen Barker Parker (4), Samuel Johnson (5,121), William Rotsler (7), Edgar A Guest (8), William Penn (9,58), George W. Childs (11), Helen Keller (12), Chaucer (13), George Herbert (14), French Proverb (15,111), Walt Whitman (16), Addison (17), Carol P. Romulo (18), Henry Brooks Adams (19), Abraham Lincoln (20), Alexander Maclean (22), Edward Clarendon (23), Robert South (24), Agnes Sanford (25), Oscar Wilde (26), Henry Ward Beecher (27,83), Robert Herrick (28), Francesco Guicciardini (29), Epictetus (30), George Washington (31,97), Ralph Waldo Emerson (33,62,106), C.S. Lewis (35), William Blake (36), Turkish Proverb (37), Colette (38), Margaret Lee Runbeck (39), Martin Luther King (40), Owen Feltham (41), Anais Nin (42), Carl G. Jung (43), Hester Lynch Piozzi (44), Joseph Joubert (45), Randolph S. Bourne (46), Wilson Mizner (47), John Selden (48), Henry Wadsworth Longfellow (49), Sir William Temple (50), Amos Bronson Alscott (51), Marion Douglas (52), Plutarch (53), Aristotle (54,59,88,114,125), Erasmus (56), English Proverb (57), Francis Quarles (60), Rebecca West (61), David Storey (63), Eustace Budgell (64), Herder (66), Edward Everett Hale (67), Walter Winchell (68), William Shakespeare (69,102), Robert Louis

Stevenson (70), David Grayson (71), Joseph Newton (72), Billy Graham (73), Charles M. Schwab (75), Marjorie Holmes (77), Pietro Aretino (78), Marcus Tullius Cicero (79,145), William Butler Yeats (80), Victor Hugo (81), Leonardo Da Vinci (82), Alexandra Stoddard (84), Emily Dickinson (85), Robert Cortes Holliday (86), Robert Southey (87), Irish Proverb (89), The Apocrypha (90), Cicero (91), Benjamin Franklin (92), Jean de la Fontaine (94), Chinese Proverb (95), Edgar Watson Howe (96), Sir Philip Sidney (98), Edwin H. Channing (99), Thomas Fuller (100), Volney Streamer (101), Geoffrey Chaucer (103), Thomas Hughes (104), Dinah Maria Mulock Craik (105), George D. Prentice (107), Christina Georgina Rossetti (108), Saint Ailred of Rievaulx (109), Arlene Francis (110), John Oliver Hobbes (112), Epicurus (113), Benjamin Disraeli (116), Thucydides (117), Charlotte Bronte (118), Betty White (119), Henry David Thoreau (120,141), Baltasar Gracian y Morales (122), George Eliot (123), James Russell Lowell (124), Lord Byron (126), Elizabeth Shane (127), Voltaire (128), Italian Proverb (129), Katherine Mansfield (130), John Dryden (131), Euripides (132), Isabel Paterson (134), Persian Proverb (135), Robert Seymour Bridges (136), Jane Austen (137), Maya Angelou (138), Plautus (139), Edward Young (142), Plato (143), Ben Jonson (146), Dave Tyson Gentry (148), Anna Cummins (150), Jeremy Taylor (151), Van Dyke (152), Thomas Aquinas (153), Alfred of Rievaulx (154).

Dear Reader:

If you would like to share with us a couple of your favorite quotes or ideas on the subject of friendship, we'd love to hear from you. Our address is:

Honor Books
P.O. Box 55388, Dept. J.
Tulsa, Oklahoma 74155

Additional Copies of this book and other titles in the
God's Little Instruction Book series are available at your local bookstore.

God's Little Instruction Book
God's Little Instruction Book II
God's Little Instruction Book for Mom
God's Little Instruction Book for Dad
God's Little Instruction Book for Graduates
God's Little Instruction Book for Students
God's Little Instruction Book for Kids
God's Little Instruction Book for Couples
God's Little Instruction Book for Men
God's Little Instruction Book — Special Gift Edition
God's Little Instruction Book Daily Calendar
God's Little Instruction Book for Women

Tulsa, Oklahoma